# Name Day

by Vijaya Bodach
Illustrations by Margeaux Lucas

“Friday is a special day,” said Ms. Haddad. “It’s Name Day! On Name Day, we talk about our names.”

"What do we say about our names?"
Matt asked.

"We can say what our name means or how we got it. For example, my first name is Noor. It means light. Find out the story of your name," said Ms. Haddad. "Ask your parents. You can invite them to Name Day, too."

At lunch, Matt's friends talked about Name Day.
Leon said, "My dad said my name means lion!"
But Matt didn't know the story of his name.

That night, he asked Mom, "Why did you name me Matt?"

"I liked the name," said Mom.

"That's all?" said Matt. That was not a good name story!

"What about Huslu, my middle name?" he asked.

"Ask your grandpa what that means," said Mom.

So Matt went to Grandpa. “Does my middle name have a story?” he asked.

“Yes. Huslu is a Miwok name,” Grandpa said. Matt nodded. He knew his family was Miwok. The Miwoks were Native Americans who settled this part of California.

Grandpa told Matt what his middle name meant. He told Matt some Miwok stories, too.

At last, it was Name Day. Lots of parents came to Matt's class. His mom and grandpa came, too.

Each girl and boy told a name story.
Then it was Matt's turn.

"I'd like to tell you about my middle name, Huslu," he said. "It means Shaggy Bear. The bear is a big part of my family's stories. It also fits me well. I was born with lots of hair!"

The class all liked Matt's story.
Matt hugged his mom and grandpa.
"Thanks for giving me great names!"
he said.